First paperback edition March 2021
Written & Edited by Josiah Eyeington
Illustrated by Gosha Bigvava
Cover Design by Josiah Eyeington

ISBN 978-1-0879-8254-0 (paperback)
Published by Matsuda Publishing House

D1518608

How to Draw Anime

The Essential Step-by-Step
Beginner's Guide

Table of Contents

TAKE COMMAND OF YOUR PENCIL LIKE A PRO!

BONUS CHAPTERS!

Introduction

What's anime?

Anime is short for 'animated cartoon' in Japanese. It's pronounced 'ah-nee-may' and written as アニメ. For Japanese, Anime originally meant any cartoon, however outside of Japan anime has exploded into popularity, all across the world. Anime now refers to the specific Japanese-style animations that we all know and love.

So what's specific to anime?

I'm glad you asked! Anime is a super unique form of animation, featuring vibrant colors, dramatic panning, and characteristic facial expressions (as we shall see in this book). It can be incredibly diverse, appealing to all ages and including many genres, from romance to historical fiction, from horror to comedy, to name a few.

Anime is worlds apart from most American cartoons. This is most obvious in the exquisite artwork, the genius storytelling, the massive variety of material and even all the cultural nuances and traditional Japanese folk stories that are often intertwined deep within complex storylines. Shows can have dozens, or even hundreds of episodes, and can suck you into a world that is far different from reality.

The anime drawing style

REALISTIC   ANIME

Anime is really diverse, with styles ranging from simple Chibi (with the childish-looking round faces, massive eyes and a cutesy look), right up to more detailed and realistic looking characters. In this book, we'll explore a wide range of different eyes and drawing styles, and we'll also cover Chibi, for all the Chibi fans out there (who doesn't love Chibi?).

Despite anime being incredibly varied, there are some characteristics that all anime genres follow. The anime drawing style was originally created to make animated characters both expressive and easy to animate. This means that many elements of the face have been simplified and exaggerated, making them easy to draw and it allows you to be super creative too!

The first most important thing about anime drawing is the facial proportions. Anime eyes and heads are much bigger than in real life, and the facial features are simplified. Lips are often a simple line and noses can be nothing more than a tiny dot!

The genius of anime is that the artists let our brains do all the work for us. We could teach in this book you how to spend hours drawing perfect realistic eyes – detailed shading, the fine details in the tear ducts, the eyelids etc. However, all of this can be achieved with a few simple lines and circles.

Here's the key. As long as the proportions are correct, and everything is where it should be, our brains will automatically fill in all the detail for us. That's right! Just one line to signify an eye boundary is all it takes for our brain to fill everything else in. Don't believe me? Look closely at some anime drawings. You'll be amazed at actually how simple they are.

Anime takes out information, but your brain still knows where everything is – the absolute bare minimum. We'll learn more about this concept throughout the book. As you'll find, it's a central idea to anime drawing, which is why we've placed such an emphasis on getting the facial proportions right from the very start.

What's manga?

Manga refers to Japanese comic books, which many anime shows are based off of. Later in this book we'll give you some tips and advice for how to create your own manga, as well as how to develop and name your own unique characters.

Why I wrote this book

So you love anime, huh? Me too! This book is for anyone who wants to draw their very own anime characters. It is written for the absolute beginner, so don't worry if it's your first time even picking up a pencil – we've got you covered.

By following my simple step by step method, you'll be drawing all your favorite anime characters in no time. You'll be amazed at what you'll be able to achieve in just a short period of time.

Just imagine being able to draw all your best friends in awesome anime style. Or having the ability to doodle super realistic anime characters wherever you are, whenever you like. You'll amaze all your friends and family with your newfound skill. This book will show you exactly how to do it.

How to use this book

I know that attempting to draw can be a little intimidating at first. That's why I've broken everything down into super simple steps. Make sure you follow each step carefully and complete all the exercises before moving onto each new chapter.

And don't forget, it's not enough to just read this book, you must practice! You can't get strong by watching someone lift weights. Similarly, you won't become a master anime artist if you don't pick up the pencil and draw. If you follow all the instructions laid out in this book and practice everything, you'll be well on your way to becoming a professional anime artist in no time!

What do I need?

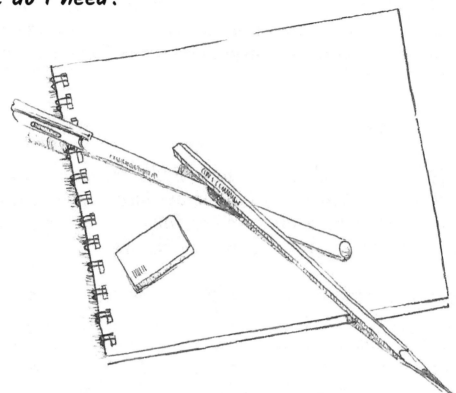

Besides having the right attitude, there are a few other things you're going to need. Firstly, you'll need something to draw with. You can use almost anything - there are no rules. However, we recommend a simple pencil. A mechanical one would be even better. They allow you to draw super lightly, and saves you time on sharpening.

Using a pencil will allow you to erase your guidelines as you draw, which you can't do with a pen. Pens do look great, especially copic pens. But wait until you've finished you're drawing in pencil first, then go ahead and outline it with a pen. You can then finally erase all the pencil marks with an eraser. Make sure it's a good quality eraser, since the red ones you get on the ends of pencils tend to smudge red marks all over your artwork, and we wouldn't want that.

Remember, everyone has their own set of preferences when it comes to exactly what type of pens and pencils to use, so don't be afraid to try out lots of different types to see which ones work best for you. There is no right or wrong set of tools to use.

Next thing you'll need is a sketchbook or exercise book. It doesn't have to be anything fancy or expensive. Yes, it's true you can draw on anything from napkins to your homework (don't tell your mum!) but trust me, you'll thank me when you have a book full of your own drawings and can see all the progress you've made all in one place. Having everything together gets especially useful when you start exploring your own drawing style and developing your own unique characters.

Take your sketchbook everywhere you go, and practice in it whenever you have any spare time. If there's one thing you should take away from this book, it's that practice makes perfect. Your sketchbook should be filled with mistakes, scribbles and experiments. The messier the better. This is a necessary part of the process. No one is born a professional artist. Everyone was once a complete beginner just like you. So enjoy this process, make mistakes and have fun!

The Fundamentals

Take Command of Your Pencil Like a Pro!

Before we can run, we must learn to walk! Let's get a solid command of that pencil. This means having your hand create exactly what you want it to create on the page (hand-eye coordination). Far too often we have an awesome idea in our minds of what we want to draw but our hands simply fail at drawing the smooth shapes and lines that we need.

By completing these initial fundamental chapters, you'll create a solid foundation with which to continue your journey along the path to mastery. Don't skip these fundamentals. You'll thank me later.

Fundamental 1: The clean circle mastery method

Faces, eyes, iris's – they are all made up of circles and ovals. The most basic shape. Practice makes perfect so get used to drawing lots of them. Even professionals will often draw a page or two of just circles of different sizes before drawing, just to warm up. Here's a few tips to get better at drawing good circles.

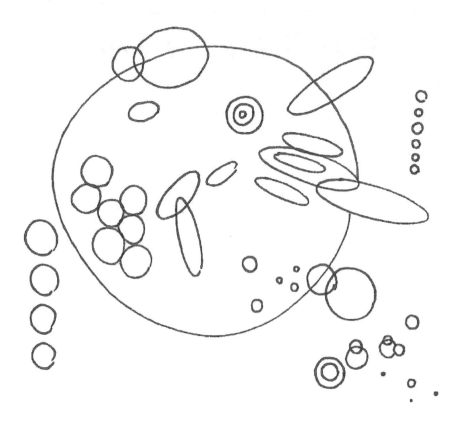

First, it's important to note that drawing is very different to writing. When you write, you anchor your palm on the page and move only your fingers. Your range of motion is very small. However, when you are drawing you should move your whole arm, hand and wrist together as one. Try it now. It may feel a little weird at first.

Don't worry if you are still a little shaky. It's because you are now using a lot of small muscles in your arm and wrist that you didn't use very much before. Your accuracy and smoothness will improve with time and practice.

One great way to make the process easier is to use two strokes instead of just one. Try starting from different angles. You can then go on to use only one stroke again when you feel more confident. Remember, they don't have to be perfect — just as good as you can make them.

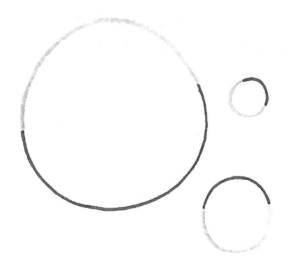

Try keeping only your little finger touching the page whilst you draw to improve your stability (instead of your whole palm).

You could also try changing your hand position to 90 degrees on the page, rather than 45. Give it a try, and you'll see an improvement.

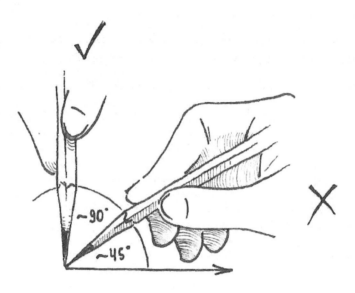

PRO TIP: Get creative with your circles. Mix things up by drawing clockwise and counterclockwise, different angles, and even circles within circles.

Once you've filled up several pages with circles, you can then move onto the second fundamental — drawing lines.

Fundamental 2: Mastering clean confident lines

First, get comfortable with your paper. You don't need to always have it completely straight in front of you. Its ok to move it around until you find an angle which is most comfortable for you to draw on, usually around 30 degrees if you are right-handed.

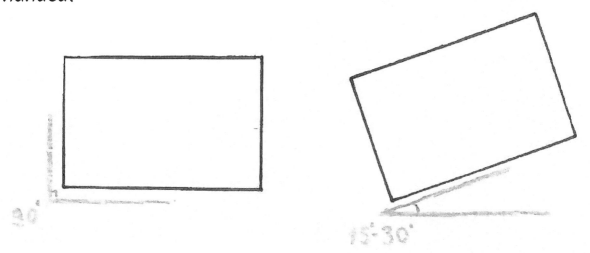

Now start drawing horizontal lines getting bigger and bigger across the page. Then fill the remaining space with vertical lines. This exercise will get you ready for drawing different sized lines whenever you need them. You'll make some mistakes to start with. Just accept them and try again as best as you can. No need to rush.

Now it's time to improve your accuracy. Draw two dots randomly anywhere on the page. Now your job is to connect the two dots in one straight line. Then trace the same line several times. Now repeat the process, choosing another two dots and again connecting them. Do this at least 10 times.

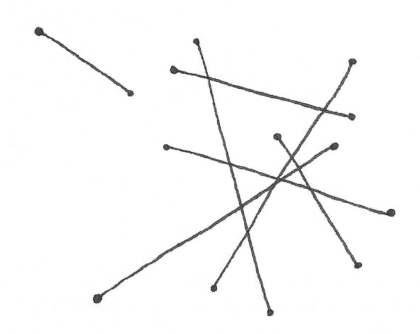

PRO TIP: Are your lines curvy? Then this means you are probably using your wrist to draw. Remember to move your whole arm.

Conclusion

You may have already noticed by now that your lines have become much sharper, and your circles much more circular. This will help you so much in the upcoming chapters. Feel free to come back to these exercises any time you like - you can never do too much practice! You hand will become more trained with time and practice, and you'll start producing lines and circles like a pro!

Enjoying this book?

We'd love to know how you like the book so far. Please leave us a review on Amazon to help us reach more people.

Thank you.

cutt.ly/Xx7xQPp
(link to review page)

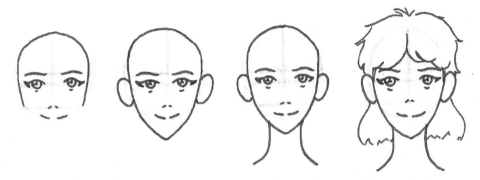

The Facial Guidelines

The magic ingredient

The exciting part! It's now time to start drawing your own anime character! :D

First we'll define all the facial guidelines to show you where everything should go, as well as the neck and hairline. Then we'll get into all the different facial features - the eyes, nose, ears and mouth. Throughout each chapter you'll learn how to change your drawings for different characters, whether they be old or young, boys or girls, cute looking or silly. Everything is broken down into simple steps.

You'll then learn how to draw lots of different anime hairstyles, and finally how to bring it all together into your very own anime creation. So what are we waiting for? Let's get started with the facial guidelines.

The Face

First, let's draw a simple circle. It doesn't have to be perfect.

Next, add a vertical line straight down the middle. This will ensure everything stays symmetrical. Then add the same horizontally.

Now we are going to draw two lines, sloping inwards, to create a more head-like shape, like this.

Let's start adding the features. The first thing we will add are the eyebrows. Draw them both along the midline, exactly halfway along the line segment. For now, we'll keep the features very simple, since we are just learning the guidelines.

Next we'll add one more line below the centerline. This is the eyeline. On this line we'll draw the two eyes. These are the eye's we'll use in this chapter. We'll cover many more eye examples and styles in later chapters. The eyes are made up of some basic curved lines and two circles.

The pupils don't have to be exactly on the eyeline, but do make sure that they are roughly halfway between the center of the circle and the side of the head. You should also make sure you keep a distance of at least one eye width in-between the two eyes, but this rule is often broken depending on the style.

The distance between they eyeline and the midline is an important distance. Let's call it x. We can use this distance to figure out where everything else should be.

2x lower than the eyeline will be where we place the nose.

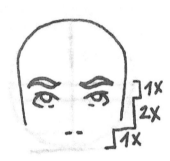

There should be Ix distance between the nose line and the bottom of the circle, where we will place the mouth. The mouth should never be any wider than the pupils.

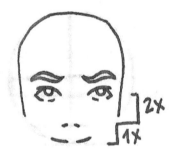

Next we'll add the chin, which should be 2x distance lower than the bottom of the circle. Continue the diagonal lines to connect the head to the chin. You can do this in two lines that meet in the middle just below mouth. This is edge of the jaw.

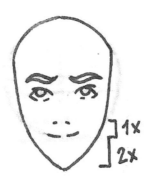

We're almost there! Now we just need to add the ears. We'll place the ears from the eyebrow line to the nose line. Keep in mind that most of the ear should fit within that circle section. Again, here we'll use a very simple ear shape for now.

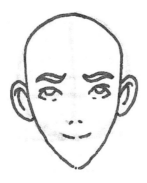

You can now go over the face in pen and then rub out your guidelines.

Congratulations! You can now draw a well proportioned face. You're well on your way to becoming an anime master.

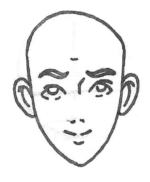

We'll be using these guideless for every character in this book, so make sure you know them off by heart. As long as you can always draw and stick to these guidelines your drawings will always look professional, every single time.

The Hairline

Anime hair is arguable one of best parts of anime drawing. Wild, crazy and diverse hairstyles are what makes anime so awesome. But where exactly does the hair line start? Once you know this, you'll have a reference point to then draw any hairstyle you like.

First, lets draw the face again, making sure all the proportions are correct. Go back and follow the steps again if you can't remember.

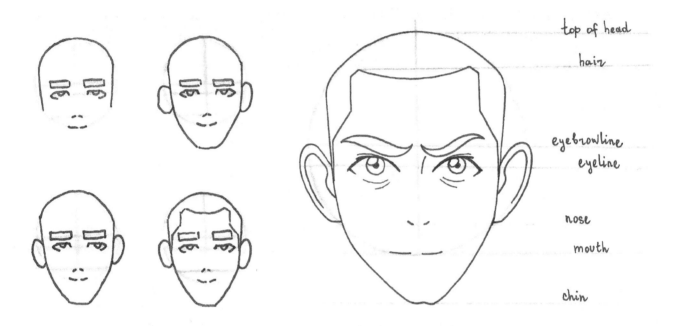

Now, from the center of the ear draw a diagonal line upwards, stopping when you reach the top of the ear. Draw another line at a greater angle that starts to slightly overlap the eyebrow. Finally, draw a straight that goes upwards. Try to memorize this kind of s-shape for all future drawings. You can then connect the two s-shapes to complete the hairline. This final line should be around 2 – 2½ x distance above the eyebrow line.

PRO TIP: Look at yourself in the mirror and notice exactly where your hairline is. Can you see the 'S' shape?

The Neck

Right now our head is floating around in free space, so let's give it a neck. We'll go over the structure of the neck, it's shapes and proportions, and finally how to draw it in anime style.

First, draw two vertical lines that extend 1x distance below the chin. These lines shouldn't extend any wider than where the pupils end.

Then draw two diagonal lines that extend at 2½x further. They shouldn't extend any wider than the ear lobes. Connect these two lines into the collar bone shape.

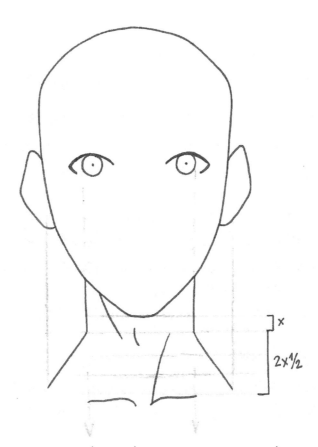

The neck has two large muscles that come together near the collar bone. These muscles are thin at the edges and fat in the middle. Two other muscles also connect to these large muscles and separate near the bottom. Further outwards there is a much wider muscle also. Finally, there is the 'Adam's apple' just below the chin. All of these muscles are normally hidden under the skin but we can still see their shape. Look at your neck in the mirror and see if you can identify all these parts of your neck.

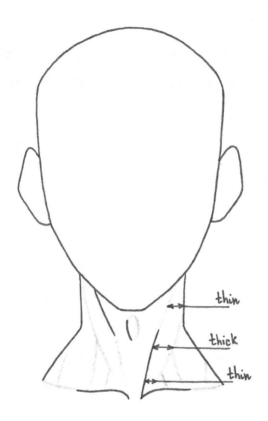

Now remember how I told you that anime style makes everything as simple as it can possiblly can be, whilst keeping all the realistic proportions? Well the neck is no different. To draw the neck in anime style, we only need to add some super simple short lines that mark the boundaries of the shapes that stick out the most.

Draw these in pen, rub out all the construction lines and... hey presto! You have yourself an anime neck. Congratulations! Practice drawing it a few times before moving on.

PRO TIP: If you are not sure how wide to draw the neck, always draw it thinner – a thinner neck is more like anime style.

Drawing without any guidelines — should I do it?

So, you may be thinking, do I really have to draw all these guidelines every single time I draw my anime characters? Well, the short answer is... no. But just remember that the number one reason people's drawings don't come out the way they wanted to is because they get the proportions wrong. It's a super easy mistake to make, and one that's avoidable.

By going through these steps and drawing your guidelines, there is no way you can accidently mess up your proportions. Once you get these right, even the most simple facial features will start to look awesome, and the face will look a whole lot more realistic.

Once you know all the guidelines off by heart, and you can visualize them all on the page, you can then draw straight away without the guidelines. However, a good anime artist is always double checking all the proportions to make sure everything is where it should be, and all the distances are correct.

Natural variations

Of course, everyone's face is different. The world would be a very boring place is everyone looked the same. Anime is no different — the characters can be wildly different to one another, adding to the overall depth and intensity of a character. As long as the basic guidelines are followed, you can play around with lots of different facial variations.

The shape of the face and neck will determine your characters' age, gender, height and even muscular build. Have a look at this face shape on the right. What type of character do you think they are?

The long face, square jaw and wide neck suggests that this character is tall, male and strong.

Draw a few different face shapes and play around with the proportions. For example, why not make the chin bigger and more square, or pointy, or rounded like a child. Try lengthening the face vs making it more short and circular. Make the neck thin or fat, remember not to exceed the eye width. Look at the face shapes below and notice how much these characters change by making these small adjustments.

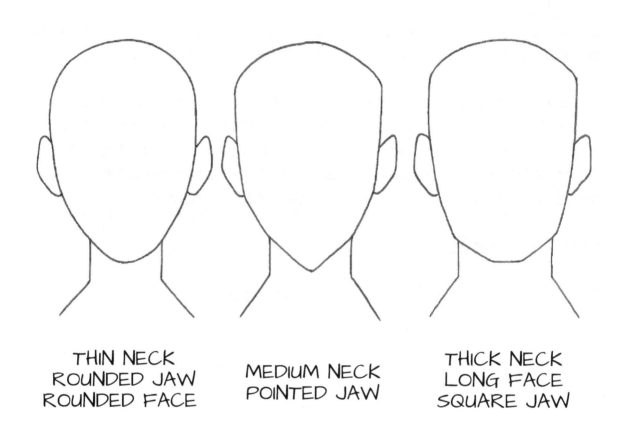

THIN NECK
ROUNDED JAW
ROUNDED FACE

MEDIUM NECK
POINTED JAW

THICK NECK
LONG FACE
SQUARE JAW

A thinner neck will make your character appear younger, whereas a thicker neck is usually for older or stronger characters. This is also true for the length of the jaw. The shorter the jaw, the more child-like it looks (Chibi style). The longer the jaw, the older your character becomes. You can experiment around with how long you want your jaw to be, just as long it doesn't exceed the length of half of your circle.

Male vs female guidelines

The guidelines are the same for both male and female characters, but you should make variations within the limits we've discussed to make your character more male or more female.

Men have longer and sharper faces than women. So we need to lengthen the face for me by making the jaw slightly longer. We'll also give it a more angular shape. For girls, we'll create a more rounded face with a smaller and more rounded jaw.

When sketching the neck, give male character a muscular build by making it wider. Girls should have a thinner neck. Finally, there are several changes to the facial features for women, such as larger eyes with more lashes, bigger lips etc. But we'll discuss these differences in the next few chapters.

MALE   FEMALE

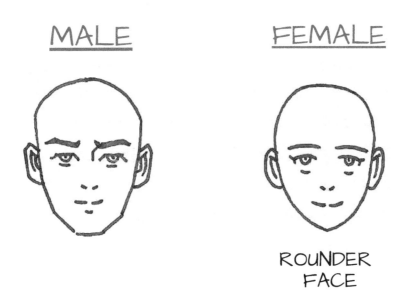

ROUNDER
FACE

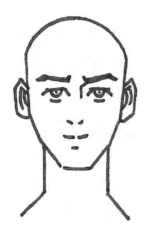

THICKER
NECK

BIGGER
MOUTH/EYES

30

The Eyes
The Ultimate Facial Feature

Now you're ready to start having some fun with anime eyes, the most important facial feature in anime. Anime eyes come in all shapes and sizes. It's incredible how much emotion you can express through your character's eyes - the possibilities are truly endless! In this chapter, we'll walk you through the step-by-step process of drawing anime eyes.

PRO TIP: To keep your eyes symmetrical whilst drawing them, it's important that you draw them both at the same time. This means that you draw them one step at a time for both eyes. Otherwise, it's very likely that after all that work and effort drawing one perfect eye, you won't be able to draw a second one that looks exactly the same.

Step by step process

Let's first start with the basic shape. Here we'll use rectangles, circles, ovals, parallelograms and trapezoids. Anime eyes usually fall into one of these five categories. Remember to draw first with light pencil.

Next, we'll draw the outline of the upper eyelid and where the eyelashes will sit. We'll also add a line in the outer corner going down, marking the side of the eye.

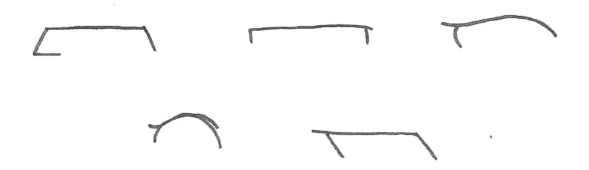

To draw the eyelashes, simply add a bit of thickness to the lines we've drawn already. In anime, individual lashes are rarely drawn, except for overly feminine characters.

In anime, the eyes usually don't really have an outline. Instead, it's suggested by the shape of the eyelids and eyelashes. Draw a line to mark the lower eyelashes. They're usually much thinner than the upper eyelashes.

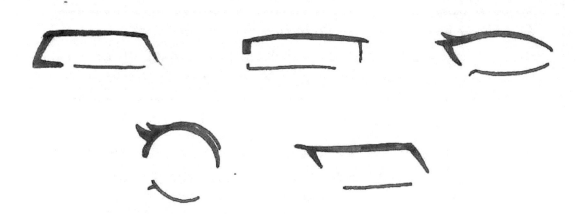

The shape of the eye is now coming together nicely. Add a thin line above the upper lashes to mark the fold in the upper eyelid.

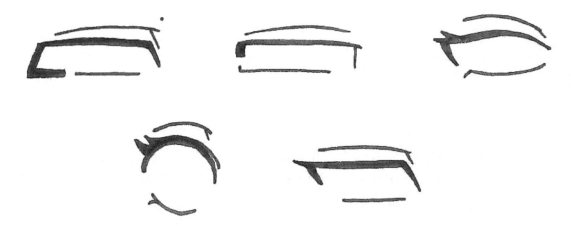

Add the iris. It should be big, circular, or oval (depending on the style you're going for).

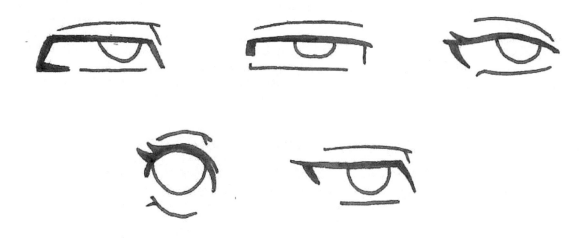

Next, add the pupil. It should be the same shape as the iris, only smaller, and it should be placed exactly in the middle of the iris. 3 pupils should be able to fit side-by-side within the iris. Also, draw a diagonal line where a shadow will be. The direction should be the same in both eyes (the symmetry is broken here).

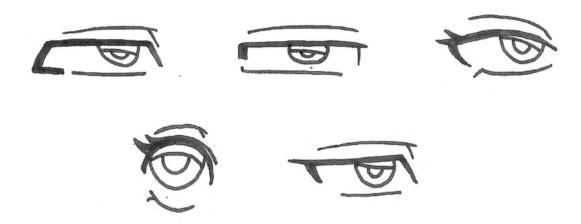

Add the eyebrow. There lots of different shapes you can choose from, but keep it simple.

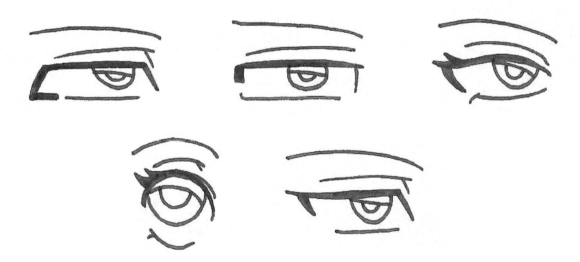

Draw the highlights. They also shouldn't be symmetrical. Draw one large one in the corner and then another one or two smaller highlights in the opposite corners. The big highlight should be in the direction of where the main light source is coming from. The small highlights are a result of the iris being see-through, it's the light going through the eye and coming out the other side. Draw these smaller ones with a much longer oval shape.

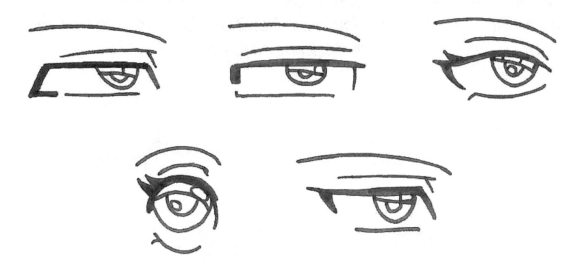

You can now fill in the outlines: fill in the pupil and the shadow, leaving only the iris and highlights untouched. Also add some shading to the iris and upper lashes. This can be done through crosshatching or adding thin lines.

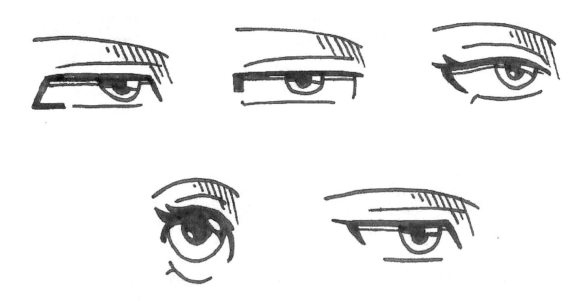

Rub out all the working lines... and voila. Now you can draw your very own anime eyes!

There's so much you can do with eyes, so much you can change and play around with. Take some time to try out lots of different shapes, eyelash styles, pupils and eyebrows. As long as you stick to these basic steps, first starting with the shape, then you can't really go wrong with anime eyes.

PRO TIP: Remember to keep them big! This is anime after all...

Closed eyes

There are many reasons why you might want your character to have closed eyes. It occurs more often than you might think. It's a great way to show emotion. Perhaps they are happy, sad or angry. Or maybe they are winking, or even sleeping! Whatever the reason, drawing closed anime eyes is very easy to do. Just imagine the upper eyelid coming down to meet the lower one, forming a single line.

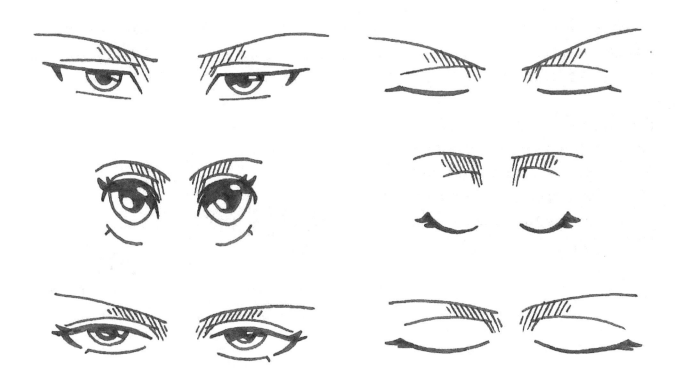

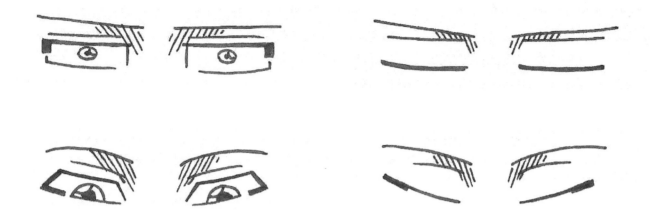

Eye variations

Your eyes can reveal a lot about your character. Is your character young or old? Older anime characters tend to have eyes that are thinner, smaller, and narrower on the face. Bigger and wider eyes, however, normally mean that the character is younger and more impressionable.

Have some fun while trying out different eyes. See what you can come up with, and then imagine the type of character they might be, based upon they eyes alone. Do they look sarcastic? Innocent?

Confused? Sleepy? Perhaps they are a villain with evil intentions - you would draw this character with very small pupils, or even none at all. This shows how detached they are from the world around them.

Girls vs boys

There are usually a few small differences between girls' and boys' eyes. Firstly, girls' eyes usually have more highlights in them, and their eyelashes are longer.

MALE

FEMALE

Some more examples

Here's a bunch of more examples to inspire you with your drawings. Go ahead and have fun experimenting with lots of different eyes. Draw five that start with a rectangle, five that start with an oval, five male, five female, and so one.

Try out lots of different ages, male, female etc. See what emotions you can discover, and what characteristics you can create. You'll quickly find out which eyes you love the most, and you'll soon develop your own personal style for drawing anime eyes.

Drawing eyes becomes incredibly easy once you know how, and they can really bring your character to life. They are the ultimate facial feature!

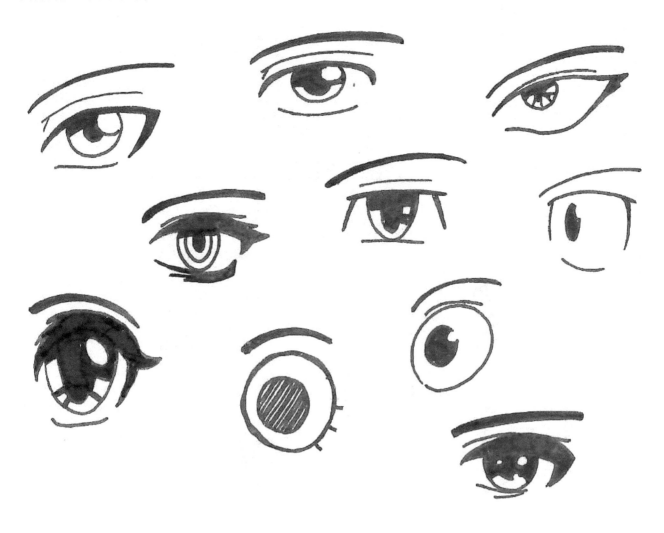

The Nose
The Simplicity of Anime

You now know how to draw a well-proportioned face and many different styles of eyes. The hardest part is over. The rest of the facial features are far simpler.

Anime noses are the simplest of all. The nose is usually shown as a simple dot or line. However, placing it correctly is important. Remember back our chapter on guidelines? Well the tip of the nose should be in the centre of the face, level with the nose line. Directly underneath the tip will be a small shadow where the nose sticks out. This can be drawn as a small upside down triangle.

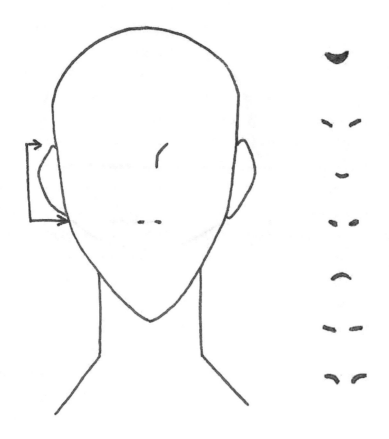

You could also leave it out entirely, or just put a dot where the tip of the nose is.

Another alternative is to simply draw the two nostrils, with either two oval dots or two small curved lines. If the character has a particularly big nose you could go as far as drawing the curved corners of the nose, however this is very rare.

You should also add a line to show where the side of the nose is. It can go on the left or right depending upon the light source. It should start next to the eye and shouldn't extend much further down than the eye itself.

Play around with a few different nose shapes and then move onto the next chapter. Remember, when drawing anime noses, it's the placement that's most important rather than the nose itself.

PRO TIP: Look closely at your favorite anime characters. How is the nose drawn? You'll probably be very surprised with just how simple it is, yet giving the impression of more detail. This is the essence of anime style.

The Mouth, Teeth & Tongue

The Gateway to Expression

Anime mouths can be surprisingly diverse, still not as much as the eyes though. When the character has a neutral emotion, the mouth is often drawn with a very simple line showing where the two lips meet, and maybe another line underneath to show where the bottom lip ends. But when there's emotion, talking or shouting, things start to get a whole lot more interesting...

First, let's start with a very simple neutral mouth shape. Again, it's important we place it correctly on the face. Go back to the guidelines chapter if you need to refresh your memory. The line showing where the two lips meet should be positioned at the bottom of the circle we started with. Rub out two small parts in the middle of this line to make it look more anime style.

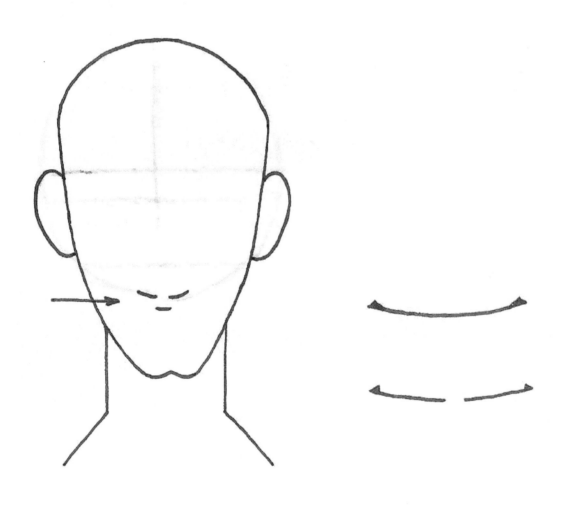

Take a look at your own mouth in the mirror. Have a look at your bottom lip. Notice that a small shadow is created directly underneath it. We'll draw this with a curved line. Add some thickness to the middle of the line to show where the shadow is.

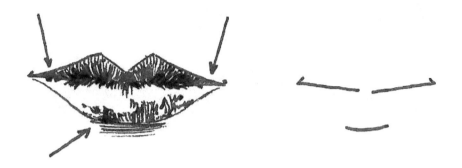

Have a look in the mirror again and you'll notice that there is a small indent above your top lip. We can draw this with another smaller curved line.

And there you have it. That's the basic anime mouth.

But what about when the mouth is open? When the mouth is open, the lips are often completely left out completely. Instead, we draw only the outline of the whole mouth. This may be in a curved upside down triangle shape, an oval shape, or even a rounded rectangle shape.

Have a look in a mirror again. See what shapes you can make with your mouth. Move it in all kind of weird ways. Can you make a circle? Now try a triangle. Then hold that position while you figure out what emotion this type of mouth might be used for. (You might want to make sure you are alone, otherwise anyone walking past might think you've gone completely crazy!)

Now come back to your sketchbook and try to replicate all this shapes you saw. Here's a few examples to try out.

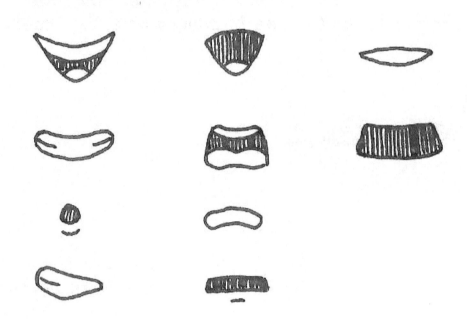

The teeth and tongue are not always visible, even if the mouth is open. The teeth are rarely drawn individually but rather a dash or two is added to show where the separation is with the upper and lower teeth.

The tongue is also drawn with just a simple line. You can then add shading. The darkest part will be the back of the mouth (neither the tongue nor teeth). The tongue can then be shaded a much lighter pattern. And finally, the teeth are left simply white.

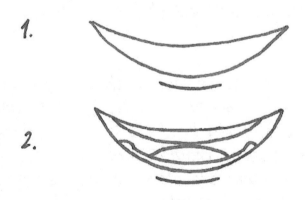

3.

You can express lots of different emotions through the shape of the mouth – the gateway to expression! We'll discuss emotions in more detail in a later chapter. For now, you should experiment with lots of different mouth shapes, with either teeth and tongue included or not

Girls vs boys

The main difference between boys and girls is the size of the mouth. Girls' mouths are normally slightly bigger. They also can have more pronounced lips. If they are very feminine then you could even draw the entire lips, though this is still very rare in anime. Apart from the lips and the mouth size, there isn't much more of a difference between boys' and girls' mouths in anime.

I reccomend you get into the habit of drawing all anime mouths, both male and female, as a simple line. Only draw lips if your character is very feminine.

49

The Ears
The Final Ingredient

In normal drawings, ears are usually very difficult to draw since they are made up of so many different parts and shapes. Luckily for us though, this book is about how to draw anime. And in anime style they are always very very simple. There's rarely any differences between characters or genders. You could make the ear a bit pointier at the top if you really wanted to differentiate your character a bit more. You could also make them bigger or smaller.

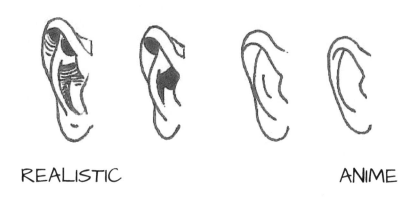

REALISTIC   ANIME

First, we'll draw the outside shape. The ear lobe has a much tighter curve than the top part of the ear. Practice drawing this outer shape with one fluid motion. You'll get better the more you practice drawing it.

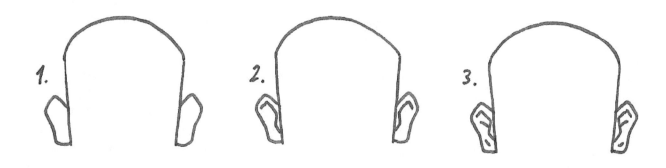

Although there are lots of things going on inside the ear, we'll only draw the main shapes. First we have what's called the tragus. This is drawn with a small vertical dash, slightly curved inwards. Then we have the conch, which is the larger curved line at the edge of the ear. These are the only two features you'll need for drawing anime ears.

Now you just have to remember to put them in the right place - in between the horizontal centre line and the mouth line. Most of the ear should fit within that small area (between the circle guideline and the edge of the head).

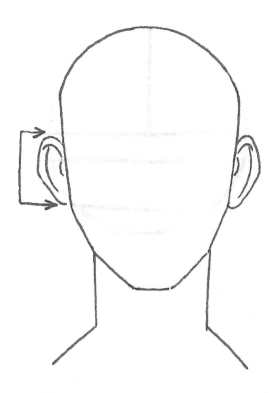

And that's it! We've now covered every facial feature on the face. Congratulations! Now let's move onto the hair, the best part of all anime drawing.

The Hair

Unleash Your Inner Creativity and Go Wild!

Now the real fun begins. Anime is known for it's crazy over-the-top hairstyles. Both boys and girls have some really cool hair. They are usually super spiky, and made up of many different parts.

It's important to remember when drawing hair that the hair is something that is added 'more' to the head. What I mean is, it should be much larger than the head itself that we have drawn already. A common mistake for beginners is to draw the hair within the head shape and to not go outside of it. Notice on the drawings below how the hair outline lies outside of the head guidelines.

First, you should decide where the hair parting/spiral will be. Everyone has one, and it's important to know where it is because it will determine the direction in which the hair goes. It's normally to the left or right of the center line, or on the top of the head. All the hair will flow away from this point. Look at these three different parting locations:

Let's start with the hairline. Make it as jagged as you like, but remember to draw the hair in triangular sections, rather than trying to draw every strand of hair. This is what your hair looks like when it gets wet, all clumped together in spikes. We'll look at both a male and female example. For both of them, we'll place the parting on the left of the head (though it could be middle or right).

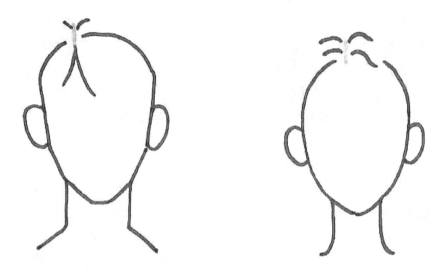

Follow the same direction as the hair guideline that we learnt about in the first chapter (starting and finishing just below the top of the ears). It's ok if the hair covers part of the eye, or even the entire eye completely! Many anime hairstyles do this.

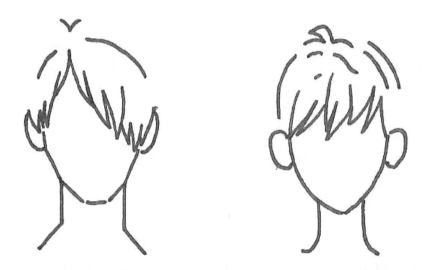

Next, it's time to add hair to the top of the head. Again, we'll draw spikes, but this time remember that they should be angled away from where the hair parting/spiral.

Continue drawing the hair that is showing behind the neck and chin.

Hair isn't perfect and doesn't all point exactly in one direction. Make sure you draw clumps that point in different directions to give it a more natural look.

Finally, you can rub out all the facial guidelines, and any facial features that are covered by the hair.

PRO TIP: Don't be afraid to go big! Anime hairstyles are normally massive, so make them as big as you like. Also, you can never have too many spikes!

Girls vs Boys

In Anime, there are normally a lot of more different hairstyles for girls than boys. Girls' hair is also often much more difficult to draw since there are more parts to it. Girls' hair is normally longer, but not always, as we shall see. There are girl's hairstyles with short hair, and boys with long hair too, sometimes tied up in a bun. We'll now have a look at lots of different hairstyles for both boys and girls.

Girls' Hairstyle Examples

Here's some common hairstyles that girls tend have in anime. We've included them here to give you some more inspiration. Feel free to use these styles in your drawings. Practice makes perfect!

Boys' Hairstyle Examples

PRO TIP: Why not draw the hair blowing in the wind for added dramatic effect? To create this effect, draw each clump of hair in the same curved direction, but be sure to make the longer clumps wave and cross over one another. The base of the clumps should remain in the same place. The clumps should also split up into smaller clumps towards the ends of each clump.

Shading
The Finishing Touches

To make your anime characters look even more realistic, you can add some overall shading. Even though our paper is only 2D, the face and head we are drawing is actually 3D. We can make it look this way through shading.

We'll add shading to things that are behind something else. So we'll draw shading on the neck, just below where the chin sticks out. And also on the face, below any sections of hair, since they stick out into 3D space also. You may have already shaded under the nose, since the nose sticks out too. It is optional to add a bit of shading to the inner ears too.

When using a pen there are a few different ways we can shade. The first is to use crosshatching. This is where you draw lots of lines in one direction and then more lines that are rotated 90

degrees to that direction. You can allow one set of lines in one direction to stick out more than the other lines to give the appearance of fading in or out.

The other way to draw a lighter shade is to simply draw lines in one direction only, and draw them more and more spaced apart to fade in and out.

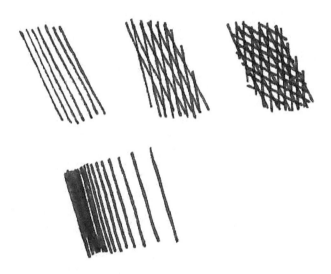

Putting It All Together

The Overall Process

I'm so happy you've made it this far through the book. We've covered a lot of content so far. Make sure you've read through each chapter, followed each step carefully, and practiced everything you've learnt. It's now time to put it all together and bring your character to life!

First, let's start with the guidelines and head shape.

Then add the eyebrows, eyes, nose and mouth.

Next add the chin, ears and neck.

And finally the hair, shading and some finishing touches.

You can use this same process to draw all kinds of different anime characters. Simply change the proportions and features to make your characters old, young, male, female etc. all with unique features. Then you can add emotion to really bring your characters to life.

See you in the next chapter!

Emotions

Bring Your Drawings to Life!

Anime characters are always brimming with emotion. These emotions are often super exaggerated for dramatic effect. It's not uncommon for an anime character who's feeling sad to be crying buckets of tears, streams running down their face. Or when they are angry, their face to go all red with steam rising up from around their face.

CRYING   ANGRY

The two main facial features that are used to show emotion are the eyes and mouth. By now, you've already drawn dozens of different anime eyes and mouths, so you might have a few ideas already.

When expressing emotion, anime mouths can get really big, nearly filling the whole face even! When expressing emotion through the eyes, you'll want to focus mostly on the shape and position of the eyebrow and the upper and lower eyelids. The location of the iris and pupil is also important, since it would point downwards to show sadness, for example. Playing around with these few components will give you a variety of different expressions to work with.

Anime gives you lots of room to be creative with facial expressions. To show that a character is in love, why not draw hearts in their eyes? You could even add some hearts floating around their head to exaggerate this emotion further. In general, if it makes sense and exaggerates the emotion, then it normally fits within the style of anime.

Below are some examples of various anime emotions. I hope they inspire you to try out some of them in your own drawings. Notice how in each example both the mouth shape and eyes/eyebrows complement each other to form the overall emotion.

HAPPY

ANNOYED/
GRUMPY

TROUBLED

FRUSTRATED

CONTENT

ANGRY /
RAGE

LAUGHING/
JOYFUL

WORRIED/
SAD

SMUG

(We'll cover emotions even more in the chibi chapter)

Common Mistakes
(and How to Avoid Them)

Mistake Number 1 -> Confusing other styles with anime

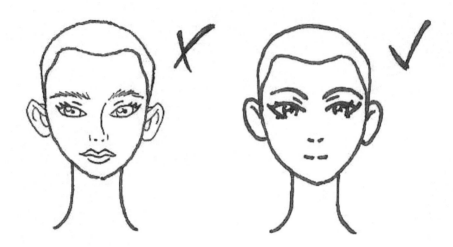

You may find yourself getting carried away whilst developing your own drawing style, however be careful not to stray too far from the Anime style. Remember, anime is incredibly simplified, so make sure you don't add too much detail in the facial features. Keep it super simple. Also, be sure to draw the features exaggerated — large eyes, over-the-top expressions etc.

Mistake Number 2 -> Drawing too small or too big

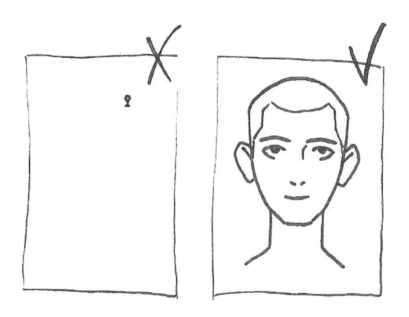

Most beginners make the mistake of drawing too small (or too big) in their sketchpads. Get into the habit of using the correct amount of space to draw. If you draw too small then your facial features will be cramped and your pen strokes will destroy detail in the eyes. If it is too large then you might run out of space on your page to draw the hair and any scenery you want to include around/behind your character. Using the correct amount of space will come with practice as you get used to your pen stroke size, drawing style and sketchpad.

Mistake Number 3 -> Shaky, wobbly or fluffy lines

If you start to realize that your lines are looking like this, go back to chapter two in this book. Relearn how to draw smooth lines and do some more of the drawing exercises explained in that chapter. The reason for the shakiness is probably because you are using only your fingers and hand to draw instead of moving your whole wrist and arm as one.

If your lines are fluffy, then you are probably doing lots of smaller strokes instead one continuous stroke. Avoid this trap! It not only gives you uneven looking lines but is also much slower. Finally, remember not to overlap your lines when it is not necessary.

Mistake Number 4 -> Uneven face shape, incorrect proportions

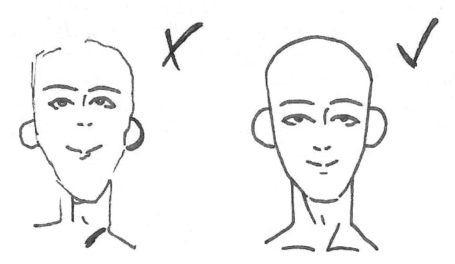

This is very easily done, especially if you start drawing without facial guidelines. If you start to notice that your drawings start to look strange or unrealistic, then you may have a problem with the proportions. Go back to chapter three and get used to drawing the guidelines again. If you initial circle is wonky then practice drawing more circles until you are happy that they are round enough.

Chibis

How to Draw in Adorable Chibi Style

'Chibi' is used to describe a specific style of anime that features characters that are short and chubby. These characters have overly exaggerated features such as massive round heads and giant eyes, making them look super cute. It also allows for them to be really expressive, with lots of over-the-top emotions and unique personalities.

Here's a chibi drawing alongside a usual anime drawing. Notice how the eyes are very different. They are rounder and far bigger. Also, notice how the rest of the features are simplified even further.

Chibi Eyes

Instead of starting with the S shapes we used previously, we will instead always start with a vertical oval for Chibi eyes.

We can then add the upper and lower eyelashes.

The pupil is exactly the same shape as the oval, only smaller. Now we'll add the pupils, reflection marks and shading.

Here are some different variations to play around with:

How to draw a chibi character step by step

Start with a semi-circle to mark the top of the head. Then draw the jaw line and chin. The chin is far smaller than in normal anime. Next, draw the two centerlines - horizontally and vertically.

Now add another guideline that is halfway between the chin and the horizontal centerline. Half this distance again and draw in another line. This distance is 'x'. Draw another line 'x' distance above the horizontal centreline.

You can now add the eyes, eyebrows, mouth and eyes (on their given lines). The nose is left out entirely when drawing chibi. The mouth should be very small and simple, lying on the vertical centerline, and halfway between the chin and quarterline. The ears should fill the whole segment, and the eyebrows can go anywhere above the eyes. The eyes should fill the whole segment.

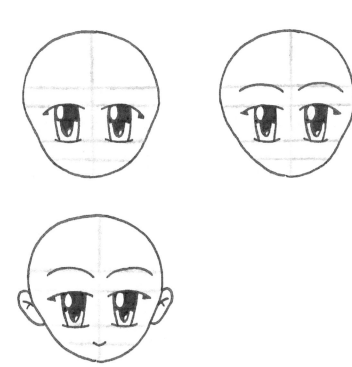

Now you can add the neck. The neck is very simple – only two lines. Make sure it is very thin to make your chibi character look extra cute.

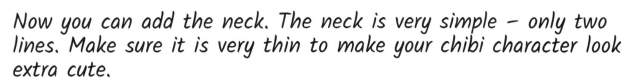

Next we need to add the hair. Chibi hair is often as big and exaggerated as the head and eyes. Remember we need to add 'more' to the head shape. Start with the top of the head, then move to the fringe, and finally the hair that falls behind the head and neck.

Chibi Emotions

As we discussed already, emotion comes mainly from the eyes. The mouth also plays a big role, along with the eyebrows. Here's some common ways you can express emotion in your chibi drawings:

CONFUSED/
DAZED

CRYING

EVIL
LAUGHTER

TIRED/
IRRITATED

SURPRISED

BORED

SMUG

HAPPY

SAD

Character Creation

Creating and Naming Your Own Manga Character

You can take your drawings to a whole new level by developing your own unique anime characters. Creating new characters is both great fun and necessary before moving onto any manga or anime design. Once you know your characters well your imagination will be set on fire will all kinds of possible storylines and how your characters will think and act within the events of the storyline. In this chapter we'll go through a few basic tips for how to develop and name your own anime character.

First, decide how old your character is. Are they an old lady, a young kid, or a middle-aged parent? Are they a boy or girl? What is their life situation, do they go to school or do they have a job? What job? What are their hobbies or habits? Write down all your ideas as you go along. You can always go back and change them if you think of something better or more interesting. At this point you can start making some sketches of how they might look.

PRO TIP: A lot of writers base their characters on a real life person. You don't have to make everything the same. You can change the name etc. but it helps to have a clear idea in your mind if you can think of someone you've met or know well.

Personality & Blood Type

Next, think about what their personality traits are. Everyone has a different personality and acts in a different way. Are they quiet and thoughtful, or loud and talkative? Are they stubborn or easily influenced? Do they work with clear logical plans or are super spontaneous, making it up as they go along? In Japan, personality is often linked to a character's blood type. To help you decide on your characters personality, you can decide which one of these four blood types your character would fall into:

<u>O blood types</u> are considered generally optimistic (rakkanshugi in Japanese). They're born leaders who are realistic and always willing to take charge and set the tone of a group. They like to look after people, especially those younger than them.

<u>A types</u> are said to be well-organized, neat, timid, mild-mannered, reliable, shy, polite, and conscientious. These qualities make them solid team players, but within reason, as type As have a tendency to get easily stressed out.

Creative and passionate but undeniably selfish are the three most striking indicators of a <u>B blood type</u>. They're curious and always want to learn new things, but at the same time, they don't want to follow the rules. The polar opposite of A types, Bs are irresponsible and lose interest in things easily.

ABs are a combination of, yes, you guessed it — blood types A and B. They're the blood type version of the zodiac Gemini; two rather distinct personalities mixed into one interesting package. These folks are hard to read, and many even say a bit odd — but that's what gives them such a mysterious, cool vibe. Given that AB is the rarest blood type in Japan, it's easy to dismiss them as eccentric or offbeat.

Naming Your Character

Now it's time to give your character a name. Why not use a Japanese name like Sakura, Ami, Mai or Yuki? But you also don't have to use a normal sounding name either. Why not think of a name that reflects their personality type? If they are a happy and joyful character, why not translate 'sun' into Japanese and call them Taiyo (太陽)? You could also name them off different Japanese Gods such as Fūjin (風神) the god of wind, or Hachiman (八幡神) the god of war.

Manga Creation

Tips for Creating Your Own Manga Comic Book

So you've got this far, developed your own unique drawing style and developed a new character or two. You're probably now dreaming of holding your very own self-made manga book with both hands and showing it off to all your friends. That might even be why you picked up this book in the first place! The main aim of this book was to teach you how to draw anime faces, but don't worry, in this chapter we'll go through everything you should know before creating your own manga.

1) Decide which characters you'll include, who is the main character and where the story is set. Which country are they in? Are they in the city or the countryside?

2) Decide how the story will finish. Where do you want your main character to end up? What have they learnt throughout the story? What will they have achieved and how have they changed? It helps to have an end goal in mind.

3) Now decide how your character starts. For example, if the story ends with your character working for an evil organization to rule the world you might want to start them off as an innocent teenager who was kind but desperate for a way to fight back to his school bullies.

4) Finally, decide how they got to the end point. Something must happen to them that shakes up their life and changes them. Perhaps they meet someone, or there's a natural disaster. How do they react? What do they do? Do they take a leap of faith or run away?

5) Take some time to imagine lots of different possibilities and write down your ideas. Once you have a basic plotline you can then break the story down into individual scenes and start writing a script of what the characters say to each other and what happens in each scene.

Manga Speech Bubbles

The Key to Dialogue

In manga, you can show that a character is thinking or saying something by using a speech bubble. Not everything is said the same way though, sometimes the character might shout, whisper, or talk with pauses between certain words or sentences. Manga style has a great way of showing these through the type of speech bubble used. There are loads of different types but we'll show you some of the main ones in this chapter.

Normal Speech Bubble

This is used for normal speech, and
can be a tall oval or wide oval, depending on how much   space there is on the page.

Double-Bubble

This type of bubble is used to create a pause between sentences or words. Simply write each part in each bubble.

Yelling Bubble

This bubble is used when a character is shouting or yelling at the top of their voice. It is draw with sharp, spiky edges.

Dashed Bubble

If the character is whispering, the bubble should be drawn with dashes instead of a solid line.

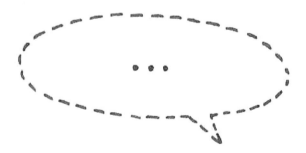

Thinking Bubble

If the character is thinking, then the bubble should be a simple oval with nothing pointing out of the circle.

Narration

You can tell the reader what is happening through the narration. The narration is written in a square/rectangular bubble.

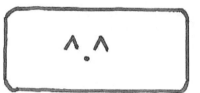

Negative Bubble

A negative bubble is often used for villains, or when a character is thinking of speaking negative thoughts about someone or something.

Final Words

I want to thank you so much for completing this book.

If you've got this far then you're amazing! A massive well done! Let's take a moment to appreciate just how far you've come.

From a total beginner, you've learnt how to take control of your pencil and draw smooth lines, circles and shapes. You then discovered the key to all professional anime drawings - starting with guidelines. We walked you through every step of the way as you mastered each facial feature, then how to shade effectively, add emotions and lots of different cool hairstyles.

But you didn't just stop there. You created your own anime characters with their own unique name and personality, based on the Japanese blood type theory. You then learnt some manga story creation fundamentals, as well as some speech bubbles that are common to manga. You're well on your way to becoming a fully fledged anime/manga artist!

However, there's plenty more skills for you to master if you want to continue improving your anime drawing ability. Perspective drawing is one such drawing technique that will help you a lot as you draw more and more in 3D. This is when you start considering the angle of the viewer and how things are smaller further away.

You'll also want to start studying some human anatomy. You don't need to be a doctor but you'll need to know the basic proportions and placements of different body parts in order to draw them accurately, just like we've done in this book already with the facial guidelines. Anime body parts are often exaggerated but overall anime and manga characters are still based on real human anatomy. You can apply the same method.

Some additional skills include: Learning how to shade in lots of different lighting situations, drawing movement and action scenes, using color effectively to bring your drawings to life, and many more.

One of the best ways to learn is to simply copy the work of real anime artists. Find some manga that you love and study the drawing techniques they use to achieve the desired effects. And get used to using a reference image when drawing your own characters. Even if you are not drawing everything based off the image, you'll still want to copy certain features, like the shading technique they use, or the style of the eyes, or how they've drawn movement in the hair etc.

And finally, be patient and don't give up! Learning to draw is not easy. We've done everything we can to make this book as easy to follow as possible, however it still takes a lot of hard work and dedication. But don't worry. It'll be extremely rewarding to see yourself gradually improve. If your drawing doesn't come out the way you want it to, then don't let it get you down. Instead try something else and come back to it. Find more inspiration from different anime and manga, choose a new character to draw, or perhaps experiment with some different facial features or hairstyles – the possibilities are truly endless!

Good luck along your path to anime drawing mastery, and have fun!

BONUS CHAPTER! -> MY FIRST MANGA

So you wanna create your own Manga, huh? Now is your chance!

On the next 6 pages I've provided you with a template for you to create your own manga. You just need to come up with a title, a clever storyline, incorporate some awesome action scenes and interesting characters and then you're all set. Cut the pages out, staple them together and then you can show off to everyone your first ever manga!

Take some time first to plan it all out before you get started, and I recommend that you draw everything first in pencil so you can rub it out if you make a mistake.

And once you're finished, go ahead and post some pictures of your finished manga into our Facebook group - we'd love to see it!! The page is called 'My First Manga' (you should be able to find it with a quick Facebook search).

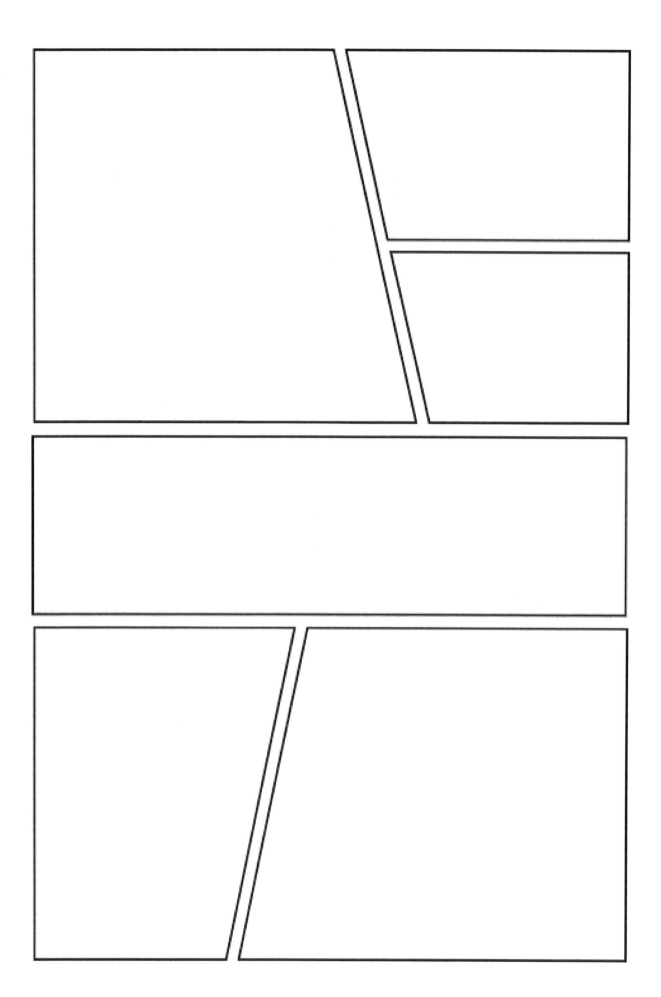

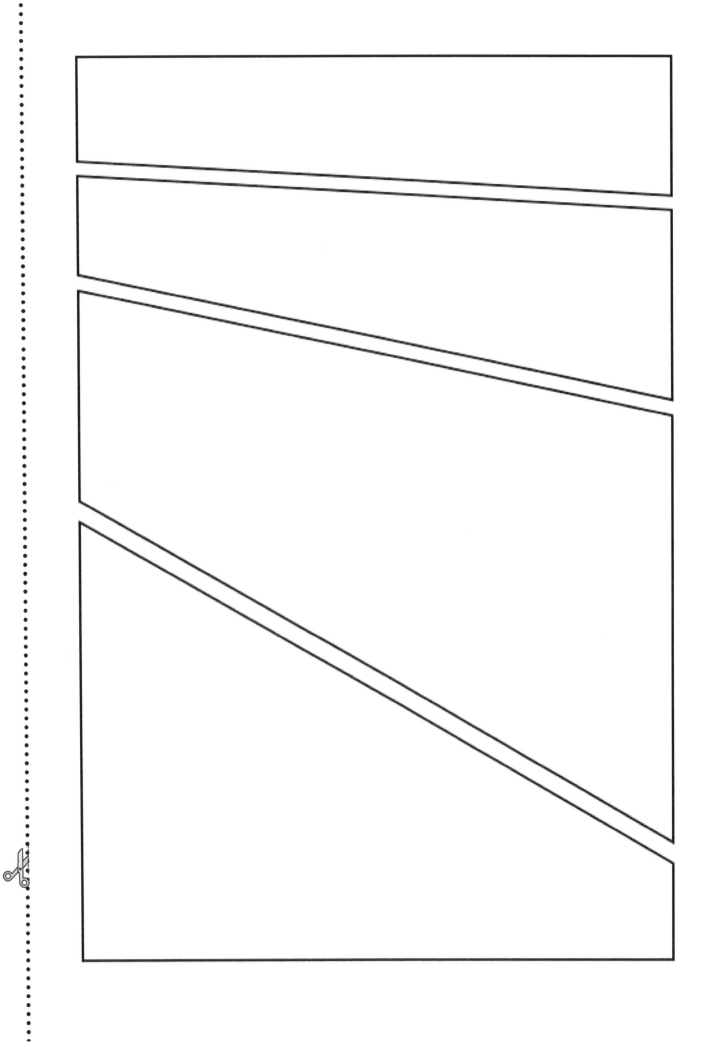

Oh, one more thing... Would you like to receive all our future books for free?

Before we release a new book, we always send out free copies to our most loyal customers to get some initial feedback and reviews. If you'd like to be part of this exclusive group, please enter your email using the link below (or QR code):

cutt.ly/ox7cdi0
(link to google form)

(We never send spam or junk mail)

Want to create more Manga?

Don't worry, we've got you covered...

Grab a copy of our 'Blank Manga Book' for endless creative fun!

Each page has a new layout, sparking new ideas for storylines, action scenes, dialogues and more! All in original Manga style.

Search "Matsuda Publishing' into Amazon to find it.

CPSIA information can be obtained
at www.ICGtesting.com
Printed in the USA
LVHW060215281222
736061LV00015B/740